Touring Japan in English

英語で学ぶ日本三選

Toshiyuki Sakabe

Noriaki Okajima

William Noel

Nan'un-do

Touring Japan in English

Copyright © 2015
by Toshiyuki Sakabe, Noriaki Okajima, William Noel

All Rights Reserved
No part of this book may be reproduced in any form
without written permission from the authors and Nan'un-do Co.,Ltd.

photo:

p.10	Chiharu / Shutterstock.com
p.11	Ivan Cheung / Shutterstock.com
p.12	Kandamyoujin
p.16	Mount Haku from Onanjimine 2011-07-17/Alpsdake
p.18	shutterstock
p.19	Arima Onsen Yumotozaka01s3200/663highland
p.23	cowardlion / Shutterstock.com
p.24	Kairakuen
p.38	Ryuusendou
p.39	Ryugadou
p.40	Akiyoshido
p.46	Fukuroda-no-taki/Mchew
p.50	Sean Pavone / Shutterstock.com
p.54	Ikameshi Abeshoten Co., Ltd
p.55	Oginoya Co., Ltd
p.56	MINAMOTO Co., Ltd
p.60	Mizusawa Udon Tamaruya/NY066
p.62	Perati Komson / Shutterstock.com
p.64	Supachita Ae / Shutterstock.com

はじめに

　2013年9月アルゼンチンで開催された国際オリンピック委員会（IOC）総会において、東京が2020年のオリンピック・パラリンピック競技大会の開催都市に選ばれました。また、日本政府観光局（JNTO）の統計によると、2013年に日本を訪れた外国人旅行者の数が初めて1000万の大台を突破しました。「観光立国」を目指す政府の施策によると、2020年までに訪日外国人旅行者数を倍増の「2000万人」とする目標を掲げています。

　このような社会情勢を背景に、現代の日本社会ではこれまでにもまして、国際社会で主体的に活躍できる学生の育成が求められています。世界で活躍する国際人に近づくためには、語学力に加えて、自国の文化や歴史に対する造詣を深めることも大切なことと考えます。

　本テキストは、これらのことを念頭に、学生一人一人が語学の学習を通し、自国の文化・歴史に更なる興味が抱けるよう配慮しております。全14章各章4ページの本書は、ワンセメスター用大学教材として使えるよう構成されています。

　なお、本テキストに掲載されているものは、具体的な調査に基づく番付の上位三つではありません。複数説あるものは、それらについてクラスの中で話し合ったりしてみるのも良いでしょう。

　最後になりましたが、本書出版にあたり快く写真を提供下さいました多くの企業に、また企画の段階から的確なアドバイスを頂きました南雲堂・原島亮氏に心から御礼申し上げます。

2014年夏　著者一同

このテキストの音声を無料で視聴（ストリーミング）・ダウンロードできます。自習用音声としてご活用ください。
以下のサイトにアクセスしてテキスト番号で検索してください。

https://nanun-do.com　テキスト番号 [**511690**]

※ 無線 LAN（WiFi）に接続してのご利用を推奨いたします。

※ 音声ダウンロードは Zip ファイルでの提供になります。
　お使いの機器によっては別途ソフトウェア（アプリケーション）の導入が必要となります。

音声ファイル
無料 DL
のご案内

※ Touring Japan in English の音声ダウンロードページは
　以下の QR コードからもご利用になれます。

Contents

Chapter 1	Japan's Top Three Castles		6
	Nagoya Castle, Osaka Castle, Kumamoto Castle		
Chapter 2	Japan's Top Three Festivals		10
	The Gion Festival, the Tenjin Festival, the Kanda Festival		
Chapter 3	Japan's Top Three Mountains		14
	Fujisan, Tateyama, Hakusan		
Chapter 4	Japan's Top Three Oldest Hot Springs		18
	Dogo Onsen, Arima Onsen, Shirahama Onsen		
Chapter 5	Japan's Top Three Gardens		22
	Kenrokuen, Korakuen, Kairakuen		
Chapter 6	Japan's Top Three Pottery Styles		26
	Raku Ware, Hagi Ware, Karatsu Ware		
Chapter 7	Japan's Top Three Night Views		30
	Mount Hakodate, Mount Maya, Mount Inasa		
Chapter 8	Japan's Top Three Famous Foods		34
	Tempura, Sushi, Sukiyaki		
Chapter 9	Japan's Top Three Limestone Caves		38
	Ryusendo, Ryugado, Akiyoshido		
Chapter 10	Japan's Top Three Scenic Spots		42
	Matsushima, Amanohashidate, Miyajima		
Chapter 11	Japan's Top Three Waterfalls		46
	Fukuroda Falls, Kegon Falls, Nachi Falls		
Chapter 12	Japan's Top Three Disappointing Places		50
	Sapporo Clock Tower, Harimaya Bridge, Hollander Slope		
Chapter 13	Japan's Top Three Ekiben		54
	Ikameshi, Touge no Kamameshi, Masu no sushi		
Chapter 14	Japan's Top Three Udon		58
	Sanuki Udon, Inaniwa Udon, Mizusawa Udon		
Appendix	Aomori, Fukushima, Chiba, Kanagawa, Tokushima, Okinawa		62
	日本地図		66

Chapter 1

Japan's Top Three Castles

- **Nagoya Castle**
- **Osaka Castle**
- **Kumamoto Castle**

Nagoya Cas

Reading

Most castles were constructed 1._____ the Sengoku period or Warring States period. They were military establishments, centers of government or residences of feudal lords. When people hear the term "castle," they would think of a castle's *tenshukaku* or main tower. 2._____ the *tenshukaku* is only one
5　part of a castle. A castle also includes *yagura* or turrets; *joumon* or city gates; *ishigaki* or stone walls; and other structures.

When it comes to 3._____ Japan's top three castles, there are various views about selecting them. However, the selection is usually based on some standards used in the Edo period such as size, attractiveness and people who were
10　involved in building the castles. The castles usually selected are Nagoya Castle, Osaka Castle and Kumamoto Castle. Their names 4._____ their locations. The *tenshukaku* of these three castles were burnt down during wars, but they have been restored as the replicas we see today.

6

Osaka Castle

True or False

本文の内容と合っているものには T、間違っているものには F を書き入れなさい。

1. (　　) Many castles were built in the Sengoku period.

2. (　　) The word *tenshukaku* means "castle".

3. (　　) There are no particular rules in deciding Japan's top three castles.

4. (　　) Nagoya Castle has its original *tenshukaku*.

Fill in the blanks

本文の空欄に入る語を下から選び記入しなさい。

1.	during	on	of	by
2.	If	However	When	And
3.	making	choosing	bringing	taking
4.	agree	predict	break	indicate

Chapter 1

■ Passage Listening

CD を聞いて質問に答えなさい。

3　Basic Data on Nagoya Castle

1. How many years did it take to build the main donjon of Nagoya Castle?

2. Who was the last person to live in the castle?

4　Basic Data on Osaka Castle

1. Who took over Osaka Castle after Toyotomi Hideyoshi?

2. When was the Toyotomi clan defeated?

5　Basic Data on Kumamoto Castle

1. How many central towers did Kumamoto Castle have?

2. Who was in charge of building the castle?

Kumamoto Castle

Japan's Top Three Castles

■ Conversation Listening 6

会話文を聞き質問に答えなさい。

1. With whom did Takashi visit Nagoya Castle?
   _____

2. What is Linda interested in?
   _____

3. Where is she from?
   _____

4. What will she do in Nagoya?
   _____

■ Vocabulary

語義として最も適切なものを下から選び、(　　) に記号を入れなさい。

1. castle   (　　)   2. fortress   (　　)
3. palace   (　　)   4. castle town (　　)
5. donjon   (　　)   6. rebuild   (　　)
7. shogunate (　　)   8. rampart   (　　)
9. warrior   (　　)   10. feudal lord (　　)

| a. 天守 | b. 要塞 | c. 武士 | d. 再建する | e. 大名 |
| f. 城下町 | g. 城壁 | h. 城 | i. 幕府 | j. 御殿 |

■ Quiz

日本のお城は普通、その地名で表されますが、時としてそのお城の特徴をよく表す別名で呼ばれることがあります。次の城の別名は何でしょうか。

1. 姫路城
2. 熊本城
3. 会津若松城

Chapter 2
Japan's Top Three Festivals

- The Gion Festival
- The Tenjin Festival
- The Kanda Festival

The Gion Festival

 7

Reading

Matsuri is the Japanese word for "festival." There are 1._____ *matsuri* all over Japan. Though each of them is unique, the origin of the *matsuri* is the same. It's a ceremony to worship a god or gods by making offerings and performing rituals. *Matsuri* are also held to get rid of curses or evil spirits. A *matsuri* usually
5 2._____ *dashi* or floats, *mikoshi* or portable Shinto shrines, and fireworks. People's interest in religion has declined, so these days *matsuri* are mainly just fun tourist events.

When it comes to naming Japan's top three festivals, two of them are 3._____ the Gion Festival and the Tenjin Festival. However the choice of
10 the third varies depending 4._____ opinions in different places. Some people think the Nebuta Festival in Aomori or the Hakata Dontaku in Fukuoka is best, but usually the Kanda Festival in Tokyo is chosen. The Gion, Tenjin and Kanda festivals have been held for more than 1000 years.

▮ True or False

本文の内容と合っているものにはT、間違っているものにはFを書き入れなさい。

1. (　　) Most *matsuri* look similar to each other.

2. (　　) *Matsuri* were started as a way to worship gods.

3. (　　) Most people are still interested in religion.

4. (　　) The Nebuta Festival is considered one of the top three festivals in Japan.

▮ Fill in the blanks

本文の空欄に入る語を下から選び記入しなさい。

1.	careless	endless	countless	useless
2.	comes	includes	has	brings
3.	unlikely	unbelievably	unfortunately	unquestionably
4.	of	on	for	in

Chapter 2

Passage Listening

CDを聞いて質問に答えなさい。

 8 Basic Data on the Gion Festival

1. What was the original purpose of the festival?

   _____

2. When does the festival end?

   _____

 9 Basic Data on the Tenjin Festival

1. How long does the festival last?

   _____

2. What is the Tenjin Festival called?

   _____

 10 Basic Data on the Kanda Festival

1. Why did the festival begin?

   _____

2. When does the festival take place now?

   _____

The Kanda Festival

Japan's Top Three Festivals

Conversation Listening

会話文を聞き質問に答えなさい。

1. Are festivals in the US similar to those in Japan?
   _____

2. Are festivals in the US related to religion?
   _____

3. What do Japanese do for the New Year's holiday?
   _____

4. How do people in the US spend Christmas?
   _____

Vocabulary

語義として最も適切なものを下から選び、(　) に記号を入れなさい。

1. parade   (　)   2. deity   (　)
3. a practice (　)   4. a phoenix (　)
5. a legend   (　)   6. auspicious (　)
7. sacred   (　)   8. decorate   (　)
9. ritual   (　)   10. praying   (　)

| a. 風習 | b. 縁起がいい | c. 神事・儀式 | d. 伝説 | e. 祈願 |
| f. 飾る | g. 練り歩く | h. 神 | i. 神聖な | j. 鳳凰 |

Quiz

夜景に因んだ夏の夜の風物詩と云えば花火を思い浮かべる人も少なくないと思います。日本三大花火大会で有名なのは次の都道府県の何という花火大会でしょうか。

1. 秋田県
2. 茨城県
3. 新潟県

Chapter 3

Japan's Top Three Mountains

- **Fujisan**
- **Tateyama**
- **Hakusan**

 12

Reading

There are a lot of mountains in Japan. Mountains and hills 1._____ almost 80 percent of the country. Most of them are volcanic, and many of them are active volcanoes. Japanese people have a long history of coexisting with mountains. Mountains have supplied people with 2._____ things for daily
5　life, such as resources and food, so it is natural that the Japanese have treasured and worshipped mountains. People believed that mountains were places 3._____ gods lived or that mountains themselves were gods. Buddhist monks and ascetics climbed mountains and kept away from the everyday world to be spiritually awakened.

10　　The three most important mountains in Japan are considered to be Fujisan (Mount Fuji), Tateyama and Hakusan. Sometimes Ontakesan is substituted for Tateyama or Hakusan. The three great mountains are 4._____ called Japan's "three holy mountains." There are shrines at the tops of those mountains. Every year, thousands of people climb the mountains.

Tateyama

True or False

本文の内容と合っているものにはT、間違っているものにはFを書き入れなさい。

1. (　) All mountains in Japan are volcanic.

2. (　) Japanese people have long valued mountains.

3. (　) Many people lived in the mountains before.

4. (　) A lot of people are interested in climbing mountains.

Fill in the blanks

本文の空欄に入る語を下から選び記入しなさい。

1.	account	cover	give	use
2.	indispensable	irresistible	impossible	uncomfortable
3.	who	which	when	where
4.	often	never	rarely	hardly

Chapter 3

Passage Listening

CDを聞いて質問に答えなさい。

🎧 13 **Basic Data on Fujisan**

1. What happened to Mount Fuji in 2013?
   _____

2. How do people regard Fujisan?
   _____

🎧 14 **Basic Data on Tateyama**

1. Which mountain range is Tateyama in?
   _____

2. How was Tateyama seen in ancient times?
   _____

🎧 15 **Basic Data on Hakusan**

1. What did people in the past consider Hakusan as?
   _____

2. What was the purpose of mountain ascetics who climbed the mountain?
   _____

Hakusan

Japan's Top Three Mountains

Conversation Listening 🎧 16

会話文を聞き質問に答えなさい。

1. Which subject does Linda like best?
   _____

2. Does Linda like mountain climbing?
   _____

3. When are they planning to climb Mount Fuji?
   _____

4. How many people will probably be in their group when they climb Mount Fuji?
   _____

Vocabulary

語義として最も適切なものを下から選び、( )に記号を入れなさい。

1. affinity   (   )   2. ancient   (   )
3. conical shape   (   )   4. climb   (   )
5. worship   (   )   6. dwell   (   )
7. mountain priest   (   )   8. ancient tradition (   )
9. pilgrimage   (   )   10. mountain range   (   )

a. 巡礼   b. 親近感   c. 山脈   d. 山伏   e. 円錐形
f. 言い伝え   g. 崇拝   h. 宿る   i. 古代の   j. 登る

Quiz

日本の各地には、○○富士と呼ばれる郷土自慢の山があります。次の山は何富士と呼ばれているでしょうか。

1. 北海道　羊蹄山
2. 岩手県　岩手山
3. 鳥取県　大山

Chapter 4

Japan's Top Three Oldest Hot Springs

- Dogo Onsen
- Arima Onsen
- Shirahama Onsen

Dogo Onsen

 17

Reading

There are thousands of *onsen* or hot springs in Japan. Almost all Japanese like *onsen*. It is ¹._____ that *onsen* have various medicinal qualities; they seem to possess properties for healing wounds, aches and pains. *Onsen* were originally used simply as public baths, but these days they are among Japan's
5   most popular tourist destinations. Also, there are outdoor *onsen*. ²._____ warming themselves in the *onsen*, the bathers enjoy the surrounding view and cool breeze.

Whether they have knowledge of *onsen* ³._____ not, almost all Japanese have heard the names of three famous *onsen*: Dogo Onsen, Arima Onsen,
10 and Shirahama Onsen. These three hot springs were mentioned in the *Kojiki*, or *Records of Ancient Matters*, the oldest chronicle in Japan. They are also mentioned in the *Nihon Shoki*, the *Chronicles of Japan*, Japan's second-oldest chronicle. Therefore, they are said to be the country's three oldest *onsen*. Among these three, Dogo Onsen is ⁴._____ the most ancient *onsen* in Japan.

Arima Onsen

True or False

本文の内容と合っているものにはT、間違っているものにはFを書き入れなさい。

1. (   ) *Onsen* are said to be able to lessen pains.

2. (   ) *Onsen* attract many tourists.

3. (   ) The *Kojiki* is a book mainly about *onsen*.

4. (   ) Dogo Onsen may be the oldest *onsen* in Japan.

Fill in the blanks

本文の空欄に入る語を下から選び記入しなさい。

1. say   said   saying   says

2. While   Although   Since   If

3. so   but   and   or

4. honestly   doubtfully   traditionally   supposedly

Chapter 4

■ Passage Listening

CD を聞いて質問に答えなさい。

 18 **Basic Data on Dogo Onsen**

1. What happened to the main building at Dogo Onsen in 1994?
   _____
   _____

2. Where did Natsume work as an English teacher?
   _____
   _____

 19 **Basic Data on Arima Onsen**

1. Why is the Arima Onsen area appealing?
   _____
   _____

2. Who improved Arima Onsen?
   _____
   _____

 20 **Basic Data on Shirahama Onsen**

1. Where did Shirahama Onsen originate from?
   _____
   _____

2. Why did nobles visit the *onsen*?
   _____
   _____

Shirahama Onsen

Japan's Top Three Oldest Hot Springs

Conversation Listening 21

会話文を聞き質問に答えなさい。

1. What do people wear in hot springs in the US?
   _____

2. When did Linda go to Dogo Onsen?
   _____

3. Whom did she go to Dogo Osen with?
   _____

4. Did she know about *hadaka no tsukiai*?
   _____

Vocabulary

語義として最も適切なものを下から選び、(　　) に記号を入れなさい。

1. a changing room	(　)	2. a bath hall	(　)
3. a washing area	(　)	4. a bathtub	(　)
5. a bathhouse	(　)	6. an outdoor bath	(　)
7. well up	(　)	8. soak	(　)
9. effective	(　)	10. heal	(　)

| a. 湧き出る | b. 癒す | c. 脱衣所 | d. 浴槽 | e. 露天風呂 |
| f. 効能がある | g. 銭湯 | h. 浴室 | i. 洗い場 | j. 浸かる |

Quiz

日本各地には有名なお菓子がたくさんありますが、日本三大銘菓と称されているお菓子は何と言うお菓子でしょうか。

1. 新潟県長岡市の大和屋で作られている和菓子
2. 石川県金沢市の森八で作られている和菓子
3. 島根県松江市の風流堂で作られている和菓子

Chapter 5

Japan's Top Three Gardens

- **Kenrokuen**
- **Korakuen**
- **Kairakuen**

Kenrokuen

 22

Reading

The three most famous gardens in Japan are 1._____ to be Kenrokuen in Kanazawa, Korakuen in Okayama, and Kairakuen in Mito. These gardens are all large landscape gardens designed with paths for walking around.

The Kenrokuen garden in Kanazawa 2._____ 150 years to complete
5 and contains several tea houses. It also has a pond, streams, footpaths, and both wooded and open grassy areas. Kenrokuen is one of the largest parks in Japan.

Okayama's Korakuen was completed in 1700. The garden is located just next 3._____ Okayama Castle, which can be seen in the background. It has a pond, streams, walking paths, and a hill that serves as a lookout. One feature of
10 Korakuen that is unusual for Japanese gardens is its large, open lawn area. It also has rice fields and tea fields.

Kairakuen in Mito is a garden 4._____ name means "a garden to enjoy with other people". Only clansmen were allowed to visit the graden at the beginning, however, later on the garden was opened to the public. This was a new
15 idea at the time and later led to the creation of public parks.

Korakuen

True or False

本文の内容と合っているものにはT、間違っているものにはFを書き入れなさい。

1. (　) Kenrokuen contains the oldest footpaths in Japan.

2. (　) Korakuen took 150 years to complete.

3. (　) Korakuen is located next to Kanazawa Castle.

4. (　) Kairakuen was opened to ordinary people.

Fill in the blanks

本文の空欄に入る語を下から選び記入しなさい。

1.	developed	written	said	improved
2.	used	had	left	took
3.	in	on	to	with
4.	whose	which	who	whom

Chapter 5

Passage Listening

CD を聞いて質問に答えなさい。

23 Basic Data on Kenrokuen

1. How is the fountain in the garden operated?
   _____

2. What is the bridge arranged to look like?
   _____

24 Basic Data on Korakuen

1. Usually who was entertained at the garden?
   _____

2. What damaged the garden?
   _____

25 Basic Data on Kairakuen

1. When is Kairakuen especially beautiful?
   _____

2. What is the Kobuntei?
   _____

Kairakuen

Japan's Top Three Gardens

Conversation Listening

会話文を聞き質問に答えなさい。

1. What is Takashi going to do at Korakuen?
   _____

2. Where is Kairakuen located?
   _____

3. Has Linda been to one of Japan's top three gardens?
   _____

4. How many people are going on the planned trip to Korakuen?
   _____

Vocabulary

語義として最も適切なものを下から選び、(　　)に記号を入れなさい。

1. spacious　(　　)　　2. boast　(　　)
3. gardener　(　　)　　4. stroll　(　　)
5. landscape　(　　)　　6. layout　(　　)
7. tea house　(　　)　　8. renowned　(　　)
9. landmark　(　　)　　10. historic site　(　　)

| a. 有名な | b. 配置 | c. 広々した | d. 史跡 | e. 誇る |
| f. 散策する | g. 茶室 | h. 景色 | i. 名所 | j. 庭師 |

Quiz

国土の六割以上が山地の日本には美しい渓谷がたくさんあります。日本三大峡谷とは次の都道府県のどの渓谷のことでしょうか。

1. 新潟県
2. 富山県
3. 三重県

Chapter 6
Japan's Top Three Pottery Styles

- Raku Ware
- Hagi Ware
- Karatsu Ware

Raku Ware

 27

Reading

There are many kinds of pottery produced in Japan, 1._____ it is hard to choose the top three. Nevertheless, the following types are often identified as the top three: Raku ware, Hagi ware and Karatsu ware.

Raku ware is characterized by moulding by hand and spatula, not on a
5   potter's wheel. Raku ware began to be produced in Kyoto during the Tensho era (1573-1592). One way in which Raku is not 2._____ other styles of Japanese pottery is that it is quite thick and its shape is deformed or irregularly formed.

Hagi ware is named 3._____ the city of Hagi in Yamaguchi Prefecture.
10 In the late 16th century the local warlord brought two Korean potters over from Korea. This was the beginning of Hagi ware production. One feature of Hagi ware is that it changes color over time due to contact with tea or sake.

Karatsu ware is produced in and around the Karatsu area of Saga Prefecture. Its typical features are its strength and simple design. The techniques used to
15 make Karatsu ware were 4._____ brought to Japan from Korea in the late 16th century.

Hagi Ware

True or False

本文の内容と合っているものには T、間違っているものには F を書き入れなさい。

1. (　　) Raku ware is made on a potter's wheel.

2. (　　) Production of Hagi ware was started in the 1700s.

3. (　　) Hagi ware never changes color.

4. (　　) Karatsu ware's features are its complex design and strength.

Fill in the blanks

本文の空欄に入る語を下から選び記入しなさい。

1.	so	but	or	and
2.	similar	much	at	like
3.	with	after	from	to
4.	promptly	strikingly	thrillingly	probably

Chapter 6

Passage Listening

CDを聞いて質問に答えなさい。

28 Basic Data on Raku Ware

1. Where did the Raku style begin?

   _____

2. What was Raku ware originally used for?

   _____

29 Basic Data on Hagi Ware

1. What is Hagi ware known for?

   _____

2. What kind of clay is known as Korean clay?

   _____

30 Basic Data on Karatsu Ware

1. What does the clay for Karatsu ware contain?

   _____

2. What was Karatsu ware originally made for?

   _____

Karatsu Ware

Japan's Top Three Pottery Styles

Conversation Listening 31

会話文を聞き質問に答えなさい。

1. How many homework assignments did Linda have?

2. Who went to Hagi?

3. Did Linda know Japan's three leading pottery styles?

4. What did Takashi say is important to be motivated?

Vocabulary

語義として最も適切なものを下から選び、(　)に記号を入れなさい。

1. glaze　　　　(　)　　2. kiln　　　　(　)
3. earthenware (　)　　4. ash　　　　(　)
5. refine　　　 (　)　　6. disciple　　(　)
7. aesthetic　 (　)　　8. firing　　　(　)
9. vase　　　　 (　)　　10. clay　　　 (　)

| a. 花瓶 | b. 灰 | c. 粘土 | d. 上品な | e. かま・炉 |
| f. 精錬する | g. 弟子・門弟 | h. 焼成 | i. 上塗りをかける | j. 陶器 |

Quiz

茶の湯で使う茶碗は焼物の代表格でありますが、お茶に因んで日本三大銘茶と云えば、次の都道府県の何というお茶のことでしょうか。

1. 京都府
2. 静岡県
3. 埼玉県

Chapter 7

Japan's Top Three Night Views

- Mount Hakodate
- Mount Maya
- Mount Inasa

Mount Hakodate

 32

Reading

　　There are many spectacular night views in Japan and around the world. One night view that is among the top three in Japan is the view from the mountain Hakodateyama in Hokkaido. After 1._____ the ropeway to the top of the mountain, viewers can see the lights of the whole city of Hakodate and the Tsugaru
5　Straits below. Some people think this view can be 2._____ to the night views in Hong Kong and Naples.

　　Another famous night view is the one from the mountain Mayasan in Kobe. From the viewing platform on the mountain you can see Osaka Bay and downtown Kobe below. A walkway called the Glittering Path leads to the viewing spot. This
10　path is made 3._____ glow-in-the-dark material that shines attractively at night.

　　A third popular night view can be seen from the mountain Inasayama, which is located in Nagasaki in Kyushu. The top can be reached by ropeway, and you can see the beautiful lights of Nagasaki City sparkling below. You can 4._____ see Nagasaki harbor and sometimes fireworks displays over the water.

Mount Maya

True or False

本文の内容と合っているものにはT、間違っているものにはFを書き入れなさい。

1. (　　) The night view from Hakodateyama is sometimes compared to the day views in Hong Kong and Naples.

2. (　　) The Tsugaru Straits can be seen from the top of Hakodateyama.

3. (　　) The Glittering Path is made from glowing materials.

4. (　　) Fireworks displays are not visible from Inasayama.

Fill in the blanks

本文の空欄に入る語を下から選び記入しなさい。

1.	taking	take	taken	to take
2.	seen	arrived	compared	left
3.	in	of	on	to
4.	hardly	also	rarely	too

Chapter 7

■ Passage Listening

CDを聞いて質問に答えなさい。

 33 **Basic Data on Hakodateyama**

1. What is another name for Hakodateyama?
   _____

2. When should you avoid visiting Hakodateyama if you want to enjoy the view?
   _____

 34 **Basic Data on Mayasan**

1. How high is Mount Maya?
   _____

2. Who was Maya?
   _____

 35 **Basic Data on Inasayama**

1. Where is Mount Inasa located?
   _____

2. What can be seen from the mountain if the weather is fine?
   _____

Mount Inasa

Japan's Top Three Night Views

Conversation Listening 36

会話文を聞き質問に答えなさい。

1. How many cities did Linda visit in Kyushu?

2. When did Takashi go to Nagasaki?

3. Did Takashi know Japan's top three night views?

4. Where will Linda go during her next vacation?

Vocabulary

語義として最も適切なものを下から選び、(　) に記号を入れなさい。

1. cityscape　　　(　)　　2. floodlight　　　(　)
3. panoramic view　(　)　　4. seasonal　　　(　)
5. vista　　　　　(　)　　6. bird's-eye view　(　)
7. must-see　　　(　)　　8. observatory　　(　)
9. harbor　　　　(　)　　10. ropeway　　　(　)

　a. 展望　　　b. 展望台　　c. 全景　　d. 鳥観的景色　e. 必見

　f. 季節的な　g. ロープウェイ　h. 都市の景観　i. 港　　j. 照明灯

Quiz

この Chapter では日本三大夜景について学びましたが、2003 年に発表された新日本三大夜景とは次の都道府県のどこでしょうか。

1. 福岡県
2. 奈良県
3. 山梨県

Chapter 8

Japan's Top Three Famous Foods

- **Tempura**
- **Sushi**
- **Sukiyaki**

 37

Reading

    1._____ Japanese food has become more and more popular globally. Japanese cuisine was included on UNESCO's Intangible Cultural Heritage list in December, 2013. It is no longer eaten just locally. Perhaps the three best-known Japanese foods are tempura, sushi, and sukiyaki.

5   The term "tempura" refers 2._____ pieces of vegetable or seafood that have been deep-fried in batter. Tempura was first brought to Japan by Portuguese Jesuits in the middle of the 16th century. Tempura pieces are dipped in sauce or salt before being eaten.

    Sushi 3._____ in different forms. *Nigiri-zushi* has various ingredients
10 placed on top of a small portion of vinegared rice. The most common ingredients are raw fish. Another type of sushi is *maki-zushi* (rolled sushi). For *maki-zushi*, rice and other ingredients, such as raw tuna or cucumber, are rolled inside a thin layer of toasted seaweed (*nori*).

    Sukiyaki is a kind of hot-pot dish. Usually, sliced strips of beef are used along
15 with tofu, vegetables, and various types of noodles. The ingredients are slowly cooked at the table in an iron pot containing soy sauce, sugar, cooking sake and water. They are then dipped in a small bowl of beaten 4._____ eggs before being eaten.

Sushi

True or False

本文の内容と合っているものにはT、間違っているものにはFを書き入れなさい。

1. (　) Japanese food is not very popular outside of Japan.

2. (　) Tempura originated in Japan in the 1600's.

3. (　) Cooked fish is a common ingredient for sushi.

4. (　) The seaweed used in rolled sushi is toasted.

Fill in the blanks

本文の空欄に入る語を下から選び記入しなさい。

1.	Unlikely	Barely	Carefully	Recently
2.	in	with	to	from
3.	cooks	comes	makes	eats
4.	boiled	raw	big	heavy

Chapter 8

Passage Listening

CDを聞いて質問に答えなさい。

38 Basic Data on Tempura

1. What vegetables are commonly used for tempura?

   _____

2. Why shouldn't tempura be eaten with watermelon?

   _____

39 Basic Data on Sushi

1. When did people begin to eat *nigiri-zushi*?

   _____

2. What was the most common topping for *nigiri-zushi* at first?

   _____

40 Basic Data on Sukiyaki

1. What does *suki* mean?

   _____

2. Why did poor people eat meat secretly?

   _____

Sukiyaki

Japan's Top Famous Foods

Conversation Listening 🔘 41

会話文を聞き質問に答えなさい。

1. Is sushi popular in the US?
   _____

2. Are there *kaiten sushi* restaurants in the US?
   _____

3. Why do many Americans know the word "sukiyaki"?
   _____

4. What is one of Takashi's favorite foods?
   _____

Vocabulary

語義として最も適切なものを下から選び、(　) に記号を入れなさい。

1. grill   (　)   2. skillet   (　)
3. dip   (　)   4. fry   (　)
5. raw fish   (　)   6. cuisine   (　)
7. seasoning   (　)   8. batter   (　)
9. deep-fry   (　)   10. crispy   (　)

a. 油でいためる	b. 料理法	c. ぱりぱりの	d. フライパン	e. 生魚
f. 焼き網で焼く	g. 衣（をつける）	h. 味付け・調味料	i. つける	j. 揚げる

Quiz

和食は、見た目の美しさに加え健康食としてその価値が認められ、2013年ユネスコ無形文化遺産に登録されました。寿司、天ぷらと並ぶ代表的な和食に蕎麦がありますが、日本三大蕎麦として知られているのは次の都道府県の何という蕎麦でしょうか。

1. 長野県
2. 島根県
3. 岩手県

Chapter 9

Japan's Top Three Limestone Caves

- **Ryusendo**
- **Ryugado**
- **Akiyoshido**

Ryusendo

Reading

Three limestone caves are widely recognized as the top three in Japan. One of them is Ryusendo, located in the town of Iwaizumi in Iwate Prefecture. The part of the cave that has been explored extends 3,600 meters or longer. 1._____ the beautiful underground lakes, visitors can see five kinds of bats and interesting stalactite formations in this cave.

Another of the top three caves is Ryugado in the city of Kami, Kochi Prefecture, on the island of Shikoku. 2._____ Ryusendo, it is a national natural monument. At the cave's exit are remains dating back to the Yayoi period. One unique feature of this cave is the clay pots from the Yayoi period that are stuck in the cave's limestone rocks.

The third major limestone cave is Akiyoshido in Yamaguchi Prefecture. It is the third largest limestone cave in Japan and is located about 100 meters underground. The site now has a one-kilometer sightseeing course 3._____ to the public. The whole cave presently 4._____ for about 8.5 kilometers in total. The interesting sights in the cave include the Ao Tenjo (Blue Ceiling) and the Hyakumai-zara (100 Plates) rock formation.

Ryugado

■ True or False

本文の内容と合っているものにはT、間違っているものにはFを書き入れなさい。

1. (　) Visitors can hardly see bats in Ryusendo.

2. (　) Ryugado is a national natural monument.

3. (　) Akiyoshido is the largest limestone cave in Japan.

4. (　) The sightseeing course at Akiyoshido is closed to the public.

■ Fill in the blanks

本文の空欄に入る語句を下から選び記入しなさい。

1.	In case of	In response to	In spite of	In addition to
2.	Same	Similar	Like	As
3.	opens	open	opening	opened
4.	extends	explores	expects	expands

Chapter 9

Passage Listening

CD を聞いて質問に答えなさい。

43　Basic Data on Ryusendo

1. Which of Ryusendo's lakes is the deepest underground lake in Japan?
   _____

2. Why is the third lake impressive?
   _____

44　Basic Data on Ryugado

1. How much of the cave can visitors explore?
   _____

2. How old must you be to take part in the Adventure Course?
   _____

45　Basic Data on Akiyoshido

1. How was the cave formed?
   _____

2. Why are long sleeves necessary?
   _____

Akiyoshido

Japan's Top Limestone Caves

Conversation Listening 46

会話文を聞き質問に答えなさい。

1. What is necessary for the formation of limestone caves?

   _____

2. Does Takashi want to be a science teacher?

   _____

3. In which state is Carlsbad Caverns National Park located?

   _____

4. How deep are Carlsbad Caverns?

   _____

Vocabulary

語義として最も適切なものを下から選び、(　　)に記号を入れなさい。

1. compose　　(　　)　　　2. fossil　　　　　(　　)
3. calcium　　(　　)　　　4. erode　　　　　(　　)
5. solution　　(　　)　　　6. dissolve　　　　(　　)
7. acid　　　 (　　)　　　8. sedimentary　　 (　　)
9. maze　　　(　　)　　　10. underground lake (　　)

a. 酸性の	b. 沈殿物の	c. 構成する	d. 地底湖	e. 迷路
f. 分解する	g. カルシウム	h. 侵食する	i. 溶解・溶液	j. 化石

Quiz

日本には大小たくさんの湖がありますが、面積の大きさから日本三大湖と称されている湖は次の都道府県にある何という湖でしょうか。

1. 滋賀県
2. 茨城県
3. 北海道

Chapter 10

Japan's Top Three Scenic Spots

- Matsushima
- Amanohashidate
- Miyajima

47

Matsushima

Reading

Japan is an island nation surrounded by the Pacific Ocean and the Sea of Japan. Its unique geographic features consist of mountains, rivers, lakes, waterfalls and gorges. Along 1._____ these features, the four distinct seasons make Japan a place with many scenic spots where the breathtaking beauty of nature can be
5 enjoyed.

When we talk about famous scenic spots in Japan, 2._____ most Japanese think of Matsushima in Miyagi Prefecture, Amanohashidate in Kyoto Prefecture, and Miyajima in Hiroshima Prefecture. These places have been recognized as the three most scenic spots in Japan since the Edo period and have inspired many
10 artists, including painters, poets and writers. There are many poems and paintings based on these places.

Today, these three places not only are favorite destinations for high school excursions 3._____ also attract millions of tourists from within Japan as 4._____ as from all over the world.

Amanohashidate

■ True or False

本文の内容と合っているものには T、間違っているものには F を書き入れなさい。

1. (　　) Japan has a wide variety of natural features.

2. (　　) These three scenic spots were not famous in the Edo period.

3. (　　) There are no poems about Matsushima.

4. (　　) Amanohashidate is a popular place for school trips.

■ Fill in the blanks

本文の空欄に入る語を下から選び記入しなさい。

1.	down	up	into	with
2.	undoubtedly	unnecessary	unexpectedly	unfortunately
3.	as	but	because	if
4.	well	much	better	good

43

Chapter 10

Passage Listening

CDを聞いて質問に答えなさい。

48 Basic Data on Matsushima

1. How long does it take to get to Matsushima from Sendai by train?
   _____

2. Where does Matsushima's name come from?
   _____

49 Basic Data on Amanohashidate

1. How far is it from Kyoto City to Amanohashidate by train?
   _____

2. How many pine trees are on Amanohashidate?
   _____

50 Basic Data on Miyajima

1. Why have people worshipped Miyajima from ancient times?
   _____

2. When did Itsukushima Shrine become a World Heritage site?
   _____

Miyajima

Japan's Top Scenic Spots

Conversation Listening 🔊 51

会話文を聞き質問に答えなさい。

1. Where is Miyazu Bay located?
   _____

2. Has Linda been to Kyoto?
   _____

3. Why are people attracted to Amanohashidate?
   _____

4. What does Amanohashidate look like when seen from the *matanozoki* position?
   _____

Vocabulary

語義として最も適切なものを下から選び、(　　)に記号を入れなさい。

1. scenic beauty　　(　　)　　2. annex　　　(　　)
3. promenade　　　(　　)　　4. lawn　　　　(　　)
5. strolling　　　　(　　)　　6. fountain　　(　　)
7. lantern　　　　(　　)　　8. sandbar　　(　　)
9. the Sea of Japan (　　)　　10. spot　　　(　　)

a. 地点・場所　　b. 遊歩道　　c. 散策　　d. 噴水　　e. 日本海
f. 灯篭　　g. 別館・離れ　　h. 名勝　　i. 芝　　j. 砂州

Quiz

周囲を海に囲まれ、四季の変化に富む日本には日本三景を含め多くの景勝地があります。日本三大松原として知られているのは次の都道府県の何という松原でしょうか。

1. 静岡県静岡市
2. 福井県敦賀市
3. 佐賀県唐津市

Chapter 11

Japan's Top Three Waterfalls

- **Fukuroda Falls**
- **Kegon Falls**
- **Nachi Falls**

🔘 52

Reading

Fukuroda Falls

Japan is a mountainous country with relatively short, fast-flowing rivers that have formed many gorges and waterfalls in mountainous areas. It is said that there
5   are over 2,000 falls 1._____ from small-scale waterfalls with a drop of just a few meters to large-scale waterfalls that drop from a great height. Some of the waterfalls freeze during the winter, resulting in magnificent sights.

Among the many waterfalls scattered throughout Japan, there are three
10 2._____ known as the greatest in the country. They are Fukuroda Falls, which cascades down over four huge rock walls in Ibaraki Prefecture; Kegon Falls, which offers a spectacular view of snowy scenery in Tochigi Prefecture; and Nachi Falls in Wakayama Prefecture, which boasts the highest drop, at 133 meters.

Many Japanese like to visit waterfalls. You may ask 3._____ this is
15 so. One reason is that Japan has a long history of nature worship, with people believing that gods live in natural 4._____.

Kegon Falls

True or False

本文の内容と合っているものには T、間違っているものには F を書き入れなさい。

1. (　　) There are many sizes of waterfalls in Japan.

2. (　　) Fukuroda Falls is located in Tochigi Prefecture.

3. (　　) The height of Nachi Falls is 133 meters.

4. (　　) Japanese tend not to care about waterfalls.

Fill in the blanks

本文の空欄に入る語を下から選び記入しなさい。

1. bringing　　　　ranging　　　　hanging　　　　coming

2. traditionally　　traditon　　　　trading　　　　traditional

3. which　　　　　why　　　　　　what　　　　　who

4. rejects　　　　projects　　　　objects　　　　subjects

Chapter 11

Passage Listening

CDを聞いて質問に答えなさい。

53　Basic Data on Fukuroda Falls

1. How high is Fukuroda Falls?

   _____

2. What is Fukuroda Falls known as?

   _____

54　Basic Data on Kegon Falls

1. Which is the lake near Kegon Falls?

   _____

2. Where does the name "Kegon" come from?

   _____

55　Basic Data on Nachi Falls

1. Where is Nachi Falls located?

   _____

2. When is Nachi Falls illuminated?

   _____

Nachi Falls

Japan's Top Waterfalls

Conversation Listening 🎧 56

会話文を聞き質問に答えなさい。

1. What is the view of Niagara Falls like?
   _____

2. Why does Linda recommend that Takashi should visit Niagara Falls at night?
   _____

3. How long does it take from New York City to Niagara Falls by bus?
   _____

4. Does Takashi presently have enough money to go to the US?
   _____

Vocabulary

語義として最も適切なものを下から選び、（　　）に記号を入れなさい。

1. mountain stream　　(　　)　　2. valley　　　　　　(　　)
3. unexplored region　(　　)　　4. fall crest　　　　(　　)
5. swift current　　　(　　)　　6. ascetic practice　(　　)
7. waterfall basin　　(　　)　　8. erosion　　　　　　(　　)
9. water current　　　(　　)　　10. vertical drop　　(　　)

a. 滝口	b. 水流	c. 滝壺	d. 渓流	e. 侵食
f. 苦行	g. 早瀬	h. 落下	i. 渓谷	j. 秘境

Quiz

日本三大暴れ川と呼ばれ、洪水や水害が多いと言われている河川があります。次の別称を持つ河川は何という河川でしょうか。

1. 坂東太郎
2. 筑紫次郎
3. 四国三郎

Chapter 12

Japan's Top Three Disappointing Places

- **Sapporo Clock Tower**
- **Harimaya Bridge**
- **Hollander Slope**

Sapporo Clock Tower

Reading

It is always fun to travel and visit places of interest. There are many places and sightseeing spots in Japan that attract many tourists. But haven't you ever been 1._____ in a place you had always wanted to visit, because it is very different 2._____ what you had imagined and expected? There are three spots in Japan that are unfortunately known 3._____ the ones most likely to disappoint visitors due to the gap between their fame and their actual scale.

These disappointing places are the Sapporo Clock Tower, built in 1878 in Sapporo; the Harimaya Bridge, first built in the Edo period in Kochi; and the Hollander Slope, which was also built in the Edo period, in Nagasaki.

4._____ people may have different opinions about which spots should be included on this list of disappointing places, most would agree that all these places have important historical and cultural value.

Harimaya Bridge

True or False

本文の内容と合っているものには T、間違っているものには F を書き入れなさい。

1. (　　) There are many tourist attractions in Japan.

2. (　　) The Sapporo Clock Tower was built in the Edo period.

3. (　　) The Hollander Slope is located in Kochi.

4. (　　) Although disappointing, these places are also important.

Fill in the blanks

本文の空欄に入る語を下から選び記入しなさい。

1. disappoints	disappoint	disappointing	disappointed
2. with	to	for	from
3. as	of	in	on
4. Though	If	Therefore	However

Chapter 12

■ Passage Listening

CD を聞いて質問に答えなさい。

🎧 58 **Basic Data on the Sapporo Clock Tower**

1. What purpose was the Sapporo Clock Tower built for?

   _____

2. Do most visitors expect to see the Sapporo Clock Tower in downtown Sapporo?

   _____

🎧 59 **Basic Data on the Harimaya Bridge**

1. Who built the Harimaya Bridge?

   _____

2. What was an original purpose of the Harimaya Bridge?

   _____

🎧 60 **Basic Data on the Hollander Slope**

1. What did the word *Oranda-san* mean in the past?

   _____

2. Which country was permitted to trade with Japan?

   _____

Hollander Slope

Japan's Top Disappointing Places

Conversation Listening 61

会話文を聞き質問に答えなさい。

1. Where do many American families like to go on vacation?
   _____

2. What is Linda's favorite vacation spot?
   _____

3. Why was Linda disappointed with the Statue of Liberty?
   _____

4. Was Linda impressed by the Four Corners?
   _____

Vocabulary

語義として最も適切なものを下から選び、(　　)に記号を入れなさい。

1. discouraged　(　)　　2. girder bridge　(　)
3. Portuguese　(　)　　4. expectation　(　)
5. asset　(　)　　6. valuable　(　)
7. Dutch　(　)　　8. property　(　)
9. heritage　(　)　　10. stone pavement　(　)

a. 価値のある　　b. オランダ人　　c. 財産・資産　　d. 期待　　e. 桁橋

f. 石畳　　g. 財産・資産　　h. ポルトガル人　　i. 遺産　　j. ガッカリ

Quiz

期待に反してがっかりする場所もあれば、息をのむほどの景勝地もあります。次の都道府県にある日本三大奇景と称されている所はどこでしょうか。

1. 大分県
2. 香川県
3. 群馬県

Chapter 13

Japan's Top Three Ekiben

- **Ikameshi**
- **Touge no kamameshi**
- **Masu no sushi**

Reading

　　The Japanese word *ekiben* is a combination of two other words: *eki*, meaning "train stations," and *ben*, meaning *bento* or "boxed meals." According 1._____ some *ekiben* fans, the first *ekiben* were sold at Utsunomiya station in Tochigi Prefecture in 1885. Today, a wide variety of *ekiben* are sold at major
5　stations or on express trains throughout Japan. Tasty *ekiben* prepared with local specialties have even made many train stations famous in Japan. Many train travelers, 2._____ travelling for business or pleasure, enjoy eating *ekiben* while 3._____ the passing scenery outside.

　　Among hundreds of different types of *ekiben* sold all across the country, the
10　three most famous *ekiben* are Ikameshi at Mori Station in Hokkaido, Touge no kamameshi at Yokokawa Station in Gumma Prefecture, and Masu no sushi at Toyama Station in Toyama Prefecture.

　　Today, there are even *ekiben* festivals or *ekiben* fairs at major department stores for those 4._____ want to eat *ekiben* but don't go on train trips.

Touge no kamameshi

True or False

本文の内容と合っているものには T、間違っているものには F を書き入れなさい。

1. (　　) It is said that the first *ekiben* were sold in the 18th century.

2. (　　) Some train stations became famous because of their *ekiben*.

3. (　　) Ikameshi is sold at Yokokawa Station.

4. (　　) People can sometimes buy *ekiben* at department stores.

Fill in the blanks

本文の空欄に入る語を下から選び記入しなさい。

1.	to	by	on	in
2.	however	whether	therefore	since
3.	watch	to watch	watched	watching
4.	who	whose	whom	which

Chapter 13

■ Passage Listening

CDを聞いて質問に答えなさい。

63 Basic Data on Ikameshi

1. What is the food inside the squid in an Ikameshi *bento*?
   _____

2. Where was the Ikameshi *bento* first introduced?
   _____

64 Basic Data on Touge no kamameshi

1. Where were *Touge no kamameshi bento* first sold?
   _____

2. Why has the *Touge no kamameshi ekiben* become famous?
   _____

65 Basic Data on Masu no sushi

1. What kind of fish is used for *Masu no sushi*?
   _____

2. When did *Masu no sushi* become a kind of *ekiben*?
   _____

Masu no sushi

Japan's Top Three Ekiben

Conversation Listening 🎧 66

会話文を聞き質問に答えなさい。

1. What time is it?
   _____

2. Did Linda know what the word *ekiben* meant?
   _____

3. When did Linda's parents come to Japan?
   _____

4. Has Linda eaten ikameshi *bento* before?
   _____

Vocabulary

語義として最も適切なものを下から選び、(　　) に記号を入れなさい。

1. ingredient　(　)　　2. portable　(　)
3. fill　　　　(　)　　4. packaging　(　)
5. container　(　)　　6. rice ball　(　)
7. chopsticks　(　)　　8. disposable　(　)
9. specialty　(　)　　10. local　(　)

| a. 特産・名産 | b. おにぎり | c. 包み紙 | d. 容器 | e. 箸 |
| f. 持ち運べる | g. 使い捨て | h. 地元の | i. 食材 | j. 詰める |

Quiz

日本は数多くの島を有する国として有名ですが、島の数が多いベスト3の都道府県はどこでしょうか。

1. 971 島
2. 605 島
3. 508 島

Chapter 14

Japan's Top Three Udon Varieties

- **Sanuki Udon**
- **Inaniwa Udon**
- **Mizusawa Udon**

Sanuki Udon

🔘 67

Reading

One of the main types of noodles in Japan is *udon*. Udon is made from wheat flour and can be served 1._____ in hot soup or
5 chilled with cold or warm dipping sauce. The triangular zone between the three Chinese cities of Xi'an, Luoyang and Taiyuan is referred to 2._____ the birthplace of noodle-eating culture. It is said that a Japanese
10 envoy to Tang Dynasty China imported this aspect of continental culture to Japan.

The present style of udon seems to have been established in the Nara and Heian periods, when it was enjoyed in Japan's aristocratic society. In the Muromachi period, udon 3._____ to the common people.

15 Among the many kinds of udon, Sanuki udon, Inaniwa udon and Mizusawa udon are said to be the top three varieties eaten in Japan. When udon is served hot as a noodle soup, it usually 4._____ with toppings, such as prawn tempura, wakame seaweed and a raw egg.

58

Inaniwa Udon

True or False

本文の内容と合っているものには T、間違っているものには F を書き入れなさい。

1. (　　) Some people enjoy eating udon in hot soup.

2. (　　) Udon culture was imported from China.

3. (　　) Udon was not popular in the Muromachi period.

4. (　　) A popular topping for udon is prawn tempura.

Fill in the blanks

本文の空欄に入る語を下から選び記入しなさい。

1.	either	both	neither	only
2.	in	as	with	for
3.	covered	went	brought	spread
4.	comes	goes	brings	eats

Chapter 14

Passage Listening

CDを聞いて質問に答えなさい。

68 Basic Data on Sanuki Udon

1. Where does Sanuki udon come from?

2. What is a feature of Sanuki udon?

69 Basic Data on Inaniwa Udon

1. When did Inaniwa udon start to be created?

2. What is the appearance of Inaniwa udon?

70 Basic Data on Mizusawa Udon

1. When was Mizusawa udon first created?

2. How many sauces are the usual options with Mizusawa udon?

Mizusawa Udon

Japan's Top Three Udon Varieties

Conversation Listening 🎧 71

会話文聞き質問に答えなさい。

1. Where is the ramen restaurant that Linda mentions?
   _____

2. Has Takashi been to the new udon restaurant?
   _____

3. What did Takashi get free?
   _____

4. Does Takashi like udon?
   _____

Vocabulary

語義として最も適切なものを下から選び、（　　）に記号を入れなさい。

1. wheat flour　（　） 2. firm　（　）
3. boil　（　） 4. chilled　（　）
5. prawn　（　） 6. chili pepper　（　）
7. buckwheat　（　） 8. dipping sauce　（　）
9. texture　（　） 10. self-service　（　）

| a. ゆでる | b. コシ | c. 冷却した | d. そば | e. 唐辛子 |
| f. うどん粉 | g. エビ | h. 歯ごたえのある | i. セルフサービス | j. つけ汁 |

Quiz

日本人にとって桜は特別な花で、毎年開花するとたくさんの人が花見に出かけます。三大桜名所と云えば次の都道府県のどこでしょうか。

1. 青森県
2. 長野県
3. 奈良県

Appendix

🔘 72 Aomori Prefecture

The _____ in Aomori Prefecture is known as one of the top three summer festivals of the Tohoku region, along with the Akita Kanto Festival in Akita Prefecture and the Sendai Tanabata Festival in Miyagi Prefecture. In the Aomori festival, more than 20 large lantern floats are drawn through the streets. One of the features of this festival is the sight of haneto dancers, who jump and dance around floats, making the festival even more lively and exciting.

🔘 73 Fukushima Prefecture

The festival called the _____ has been designated as an Important Intangible Folk Cultural Property. It is said to have been started as a military training exercise by the warrior Taira no Masakado, one of the founders of the Soma Domain. Approximately 500 samurai horsemen armed with swords race and display various skills on a large field, recreating spectacular and lively scenes of the Sengoku period.

74 Chiba Prefecture

Most of Chiba Prefecture lies on the Boso Peninsula. Chiba is home to Narita International Airport, Japan's second-largest international airport after Haneda International Airport in Tokyo. Narita International Airport was opened in 1978 and has been welcoming throngs of foreign visitors ever since. However, perhaps the best-known place in Chiba is _____, a theme park based on the films produced by the Walt Disney Company. It opened in 1983 as the first Disney theme park outside of the United States.

75 Kanagawa Prefecture

_____ connects Honmoku Pier and Daikoku Pier in Tokyo Bay. Opened in 1990, it is a cable-stayed bridge 860 meters in length. It is lit up at night, presenting a captivating sight. The bridge is famous as a dating spot. There used to be an observation facility where visitors could enjoy a panoramic night view, but unfortunately it closed in 2010.

Appendix

76 **Tokushima Prefecture**

Tokushima Prefecture has a famous dance festival called the _____. It is held in the middle of August every year. It is the largest dance festival in Japan and attracts many tourists not only within the country but also from abroad. Groups of dancers and musicians, called *ren*, dance through the streets. The festival's origins are not clear, but it became popular when the Tokushima Domain was formed.

77 **Okinawa Prefecture**

Okinawa Prefecture is the southernmost prefecture in Japan consisting of hundreds of inhabited and uninhabited islands. After 27 years under American rule due to Japan's defeat in World War Ⅱ, Okinawa was returned to Japan in 1972. One of the tourist spots there is _____, a representative example of Okinawa's history and culture. It burned down several times, however, it was rebuilt after being destroyed each time. The present castle was reconstructed in 1992 to mark the 20th anniversary of Okinawa's return to Japan.

Let's Talk about World Heritage Sites in Japan

World Cultural Heritage Sites

1993	Buddhist Monuments in the Horyu-ji Area
1993	Himeji-jo (Himeji Castle)
1994	Historic Monuments of Ancient Kyoto (Kyoto, Uji and Otsu Cities)
1995	Historic Villages of Shirakawa-go and Gokayama
1996	Hiroshima Peace Memorial (Genbaku Dome)
1996	Itsukushima Shinto Shrine
1998	Historic Monuments of Ancient Nara
1999	Shrines and Temples of Nikko
2000	Gusuku Sites and Related Properties of the Kingdom of Ryukyu
2004	Sacred Sites and Piligrimage Routes in the Kii Mountain Range
2007	Iwami Ginzan Silver Mine and its Cultural Landscape
2011	Hiraizumi-Temples, Gardens and Archaeological Sites Representing the Buddhist Pure Land
2013	Fujisan, Sacred Place and Source of Artistic Inspiration
2014	Tomioka Silk Mill and Related Sites

World Natural Heritage Sites

1993	Yakushima
1993	Shirakami-Sanchi
2005	Shiretoko
2011	Ogasawara Islands

《日本地図》

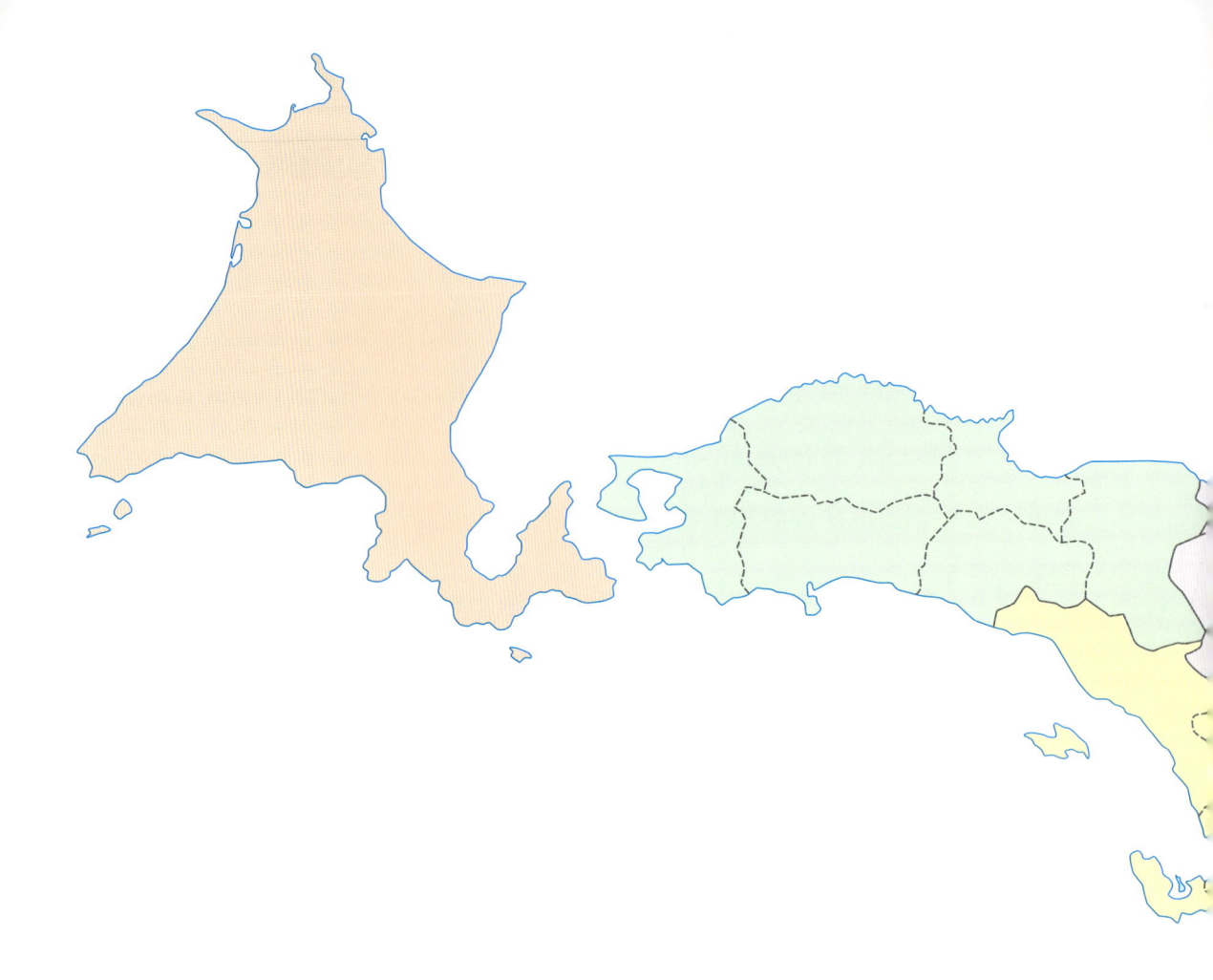

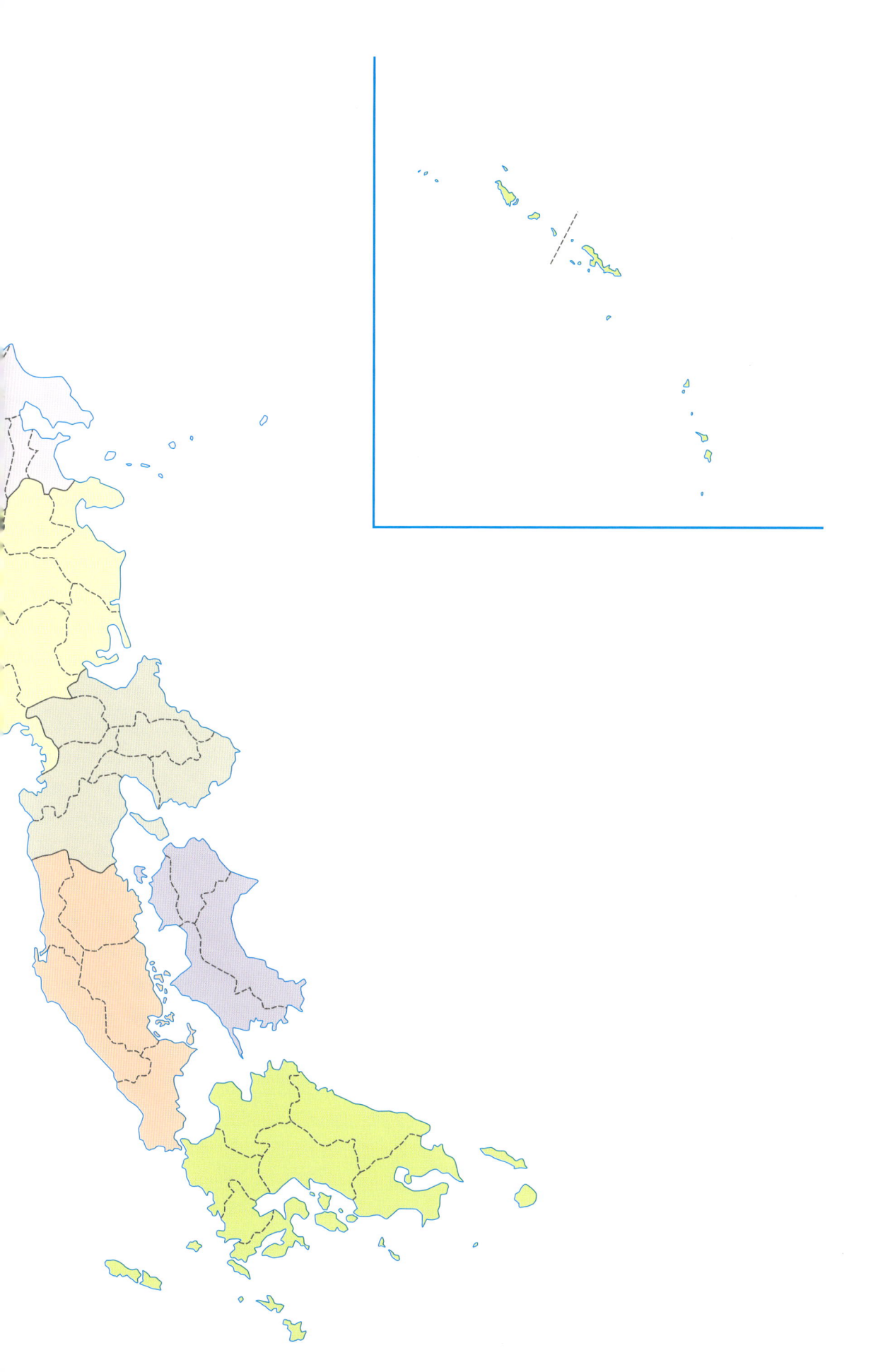

| 著作権法上、無断複写・複製は禁じられています。|

Touring Japan in English [B-788]

英語で学ぶ日本三選

1 刷	2015 年 4 月 1 日
7 刷	2023 年 8 月 30 日

著　者	坂部　俊行　　Toshiyuki Sakabe
	岡島　德昭　　Noriaki Okajima
	ウィリアム　ノエル　　William Noel

発行者	南雲　一範　Kazunori Nagumo
発行所	株式会社　南雲堂
	〒162-0801　東京都新宿区山吹町 361
	NAN'UN-DO CO.,Ltd.
	361 Yamabuki-cho, Shinjuku-ku, Tokyo 162-0801, Japan
	振替口座：00160-0-46863
	TEL：03-3268-2311（代表）／FAX：03-3269-2486

製　版	原島　亮
印刷所	日本ハイコム株式会社
検　印	省略
コード	ISBN 978-4-523-17788-3　　　　C0082

Printed in Japan

E-mail　nanundo@post.email.ne.jp
URL　　https://www.nanun-do.co.jp/